Christmas
COOKIES

Christmas
COOKIES

Festive treats to bake and enjoy

This edition published in 2011

LOVE FOOD is an imprint of Parragon Books Ltd

Parragon
Queen Street House
4 Queen Street
Bath BA1 1HE, UK

Copyright © Parragon Books Ltd 2011

LOVE FOOD and the accompanying heart device is a registered trade mark of Parragon Books Ltd in Australia, the UK, USA, India and the EU.

ISBN: 978-1-4454-3797-2
Printed in China

Introduction by Linda Doeser
New recipes written by Sandra Baddeley
Cover design by Donna-Marie Scrase and Talking Design
Design by Donna-Marie Scrase
Cover photography is Star shaped gingerbread biscuits with red ribbon, elevated view © Foodcollection/Getty Images
Additional photography by Clive Streeter with food styling by Angela Drake

Notes for the Reader
This book uses both metric and imperial measurements. Follow the same units of measurement throughout; do not mix metric and imperial. All spoon measurements are level: teaspoons are assumed to be 5 ml, and tablespoons are assumed to be 15 ml. Unless otherwise stated, milk is assumed to be full fat, eggs and individual vegetables are medium, and pepper is freshly ground black pepper.

The times given are an approximate guide only. Preparation times differ according to the techniques used by different people and the cooking times may also vary from those given. Optional ingredients, variations or serving suggestions have not been included in the calculations.

Recipes using raw or very lightly cooked eggs should be avoided by infants, the elderly, pregnant women, convalescents and anyone suffering from an illness. Pregnant and breastfeeding women are advised to avoid eating peanuts and peanut products. Sufferers from nut allergies should be aware that some of the ready-made ingredients used in the recipes in this book may contain nuts. Always check the packaging before use.

CONTENTS

INTRODUCTION

For centuries, delicious edible treats have been as integral to traditional Christmas celebrations as a kiss beneath the mistletoe. In the week leading up to the great day, generations have rolled up their sleeves and bustled about their kitchens baking – cakes particularly, but also breads, pastries and cookies.

Every country has its own culinary traditions. In France, for example, village children would go from house to house singing carols on Christmas Eve and were rewarded with cornmeal wafer biscuits, while warmer spices featured in the cookies from further north – Dutch speculaas, German lebkuchen, Swedish papparkakor and British gingerbread men.

However, it is in the United States where the tradition of baking Christmas cookies has grown and flourished. European immigrants took their Christmas recipes across the Atlantic with them and a new seasonal custom took root. Starting with the invention of the sugar cookie in Pennsylvania, American cooks have developed a vast array of tasty Christmas treats to give as gifts, to offer visiting friends, family and neighbours, to hang on the Christmas tree and, of course, to accompany a glass of milk left out for Santa on Christmas Eve.

A SEASONAL TOUCH

Cookies with a Christmas theme are easy to make and decorate. If you make a dough that can be rolled out, you can cut out any number of seasonal shapes. A huge range of specially shaped cookie cutters is available – holly leaves, snowflakes, stars, bells, Christmas trees, reindeer, Santa (with or without his sleigh and/or sack), Christmas stockings, angels and candy canes, among others. These will always be popular with children and make lovely edible decorations. However, cookies made by the whisking method taste equally delicious and, even if they're a less fancy shape, can be decorated just as attractively.

You don't have to be particularly artistic to decorate Christmas-themed cookies, just be in a festive frame of mind. In fact, it's a wonderful pre-Christmas activity to share with over-excited children and even pre-schoolers can drizzle icing and sprinkle coloured sugar with a surprising degree of accuracy.

A simple glacé icing, made with icing sugar and lemon juice or hot water flavoured with vanilla extract, or an icing glaze, made with icing sugar, lemon juice and egg white, are ideal for drizzling, piping or spreading on cookies. Both are easily coloured with a few drops of food colouring.

7

Once the cookies are iced, a good supply of coloured and chocolate sprinkles, gold and silver balls, sugar shapes, such as stars and flowers, edible glitter and even small sweets can be applied immediately and will keep children happily, if slightly messily, occupied, for half an hour. Almost as easy is to decorate with coloured sugar. Mix caster sugar with a little food colouring paste in a plastic bag, rubbing it well in, then sprinkle over unset icing or a topping of melted chocolate.

Piped icing decorations always look special but do take a little practice and a fairly steady hand. Cookies are a good place to begin as they are small, easy-to-handle and have a home-made quality that only adds to their charm. Food-colouring pens can sometimes be a good alternative to piping. Available in a wide range of colours, these look like felt-tipped pens and can be used to decorate dry, firm icing. They are ideal for writing names, initials and messages on cookies, drawing designs such as stripes, spots and stars and for colouring in shapes.

WE WISH YOU A MERRY CHRISTMAS

Iced cookies make delightful Christmas tree decorations. Before baking, use a skewer or knitting needle to pierce a hole in the top of each cookie that will be large enough to thread ribbon through. You may need to pierce again after cooking as the dough spreads during baking and may partially close the holes. Ice and decorate the cookies and leave to set before threading thin ribbon through the holes, knotting and hanging from the tree.

Cookies with a jewelled or stained-glass effect also look lovely hanging from the Christmas tree. You can make these any shape you like. For example, stamp out stars from rolled-out cookie dough, then stamp out smaller stars or rounds

from the centres, leaving a frame all around. Don't forget to pierce holes in the tops for hanging. Bake the cookies on a lined baking sheet for about 5 minutes in a preheated oven, 180°C/350°F/Gas Mark 4, for about 5 minutes, then remove from the oven and fill the centres of each with crushed boiled sweets (don't mix the colours in the same cookie). Return to the oven and bake for a further 5–8 minutes, until the cookies are golden and the sweets have melted and filled the spaces. Leave to cool until the centres have set, then carefully remove from the baking sheet. There are several recipes for these popular edible decorations in this book.

Home-made cookies make a thoughtful gift, especially for the elderly or those who live a long way from their families. Spending your time and effort baking cookies makes the gift seem particularly precious, especially in our busy modern age. To make them even more special wrap them prettily. An easy way is to cut a square of cellophane, make a pile of cookies in the centre, gather up the edges and tie the cellophane together with a ribbon or piece of raffia. Packing the cookies in an attractive storage jar makes a two-in-one present and will also keep the cookies fresh. Similarly, you could pack cellophane-wrapped cookies inside a cup standing on a saucer ready for morning coffee on Christmas Day.

A final touch would be to make an edible gift tag. Roll out cookie dough and cut out a Christmas shape, such as a Christmas tree, holly leaf or bell, using a small cookie cutter. Make a hole in the top with a skewer or knitting needle large enough to thread ribbon through and bake. When cool, ice, decorate and write your message, then thread with ribbon and tie on your gift.

Snowflake
GINGERBREAD

Makes 30
- 350 g/12 oz plain flour, plus extra for dusting
- 1 tbsp ground ginger
- 1 tsp bicarbonate of soda
- 100 g/3½ oz butter, softened, plus extra for greasing
- 175 g/6 oz soft brown sugar
- 1 egg, beaten
- 4 tbsp golden syrup

To decorate
- 115 g/4 oz icing sugar
- 2 tbsp lemon juice

1 Preheat the oven to 180°C/350°F/Gas Mark 4. Grease three baking sheets.

2 Sift the flour, ginger and bicarbonate of soda together in a bowl. Add the butter and rub into the flour until the mixture resembles fine breadcrumbs, then stir in the brown sugar.

3 In another bowl, beat together the egg and golden syrup with a fork. Pour this mixture into the flour mixture and mix to make a smooth dough, kneading lightly with your hands.

4 Roll the dough out on a lightly floured work surface to about 5 mm/¼ inch thick and cut into shapes using a snowflake-shaped cutter. Transfer the cookies to the prepared baking sheets.

5 Bake in the preheated oven for 10 minutes until golden brown. Remove the cookies from the oven and allow to cool for 5 minutes before transferring, using a palette knife, to a wire rack to cool completely.

6 Once the cookies are cool, mix together the icing sugar and lemon juice until smooth and place into a piping bag fitted with a very small nozzle. Pipe snowflake shapes onto each biscuit, using the icing. Leave to set for a few hours.

Eggnog
COKIES

Makes 35

- 1 egg
- 175 g/6 oz caster sugar
- 6 tbsp rum
- 3 tbsp milk
- 150 g/5½ oz butter, softened, plus extra for greasing
- 1 tsp vanilla extract
- 2 egg yolks
- 280 g/10 oz plain flour
- 1 tsp baking powder
- ¾ tsp ground nutmeg
- 175 g/6 oz icing sugar

1 Preheat the oven to 160°C/325°F/Gas Mark 3. Grease two baking sheets. To make the eggnog mixture, beat together the egg, 25 g/1 oz of the caster sugar, rum and milk until frothy. Set aside.

2 In a large bowl, cream the rest of the caster sugar and 140 g/5 oz of the butter until light and fluffy. Beat in the vanilla extract and egg yolks until smooth.

3 Sift together the flour, baking powder and ½ teaspoon of nutmeg into the mixture and beat in 100 ml/4 fl oz of the eggnog mixture until just combined.

4 Place heaped teaspoonfuls of the mixture on the prepared baking sheets, spaced well apart. Flatten slightly with damp fingers and bake in the preheated oven for 20–25 minutes, or until the bottom of the cookies turn golden.

5 Leave to cool for 5 minutes on the baking sheets and then transfer to wire racks to cool completely.

6 Once the cookies are cool, beat together the icing sugar, remaining butter and the remaining eggnog mixture to make a soft, spreadable icing. Ice the cookies and sprinkle with a little nutmeg on top. Leave to set for a few hours.

Spiced
RUM COOKIES

Makes 18

- 175 g/6 oz unsalted butter, softened, plus extra for greasing
- 175 g/6 oz dark muscovado sugar
- 225 g/8 oz plain flour
- pinch of salt
- ½ tsp bicarbonate of soda
- 1 tsp ground cinnamon
- ¼ tsp ground coriander
- ½ tsp ground nutmeg
- ¼ tsp ground cloves
- 2 tbsp dark rum

1 Preheat the oven to 180°C/350°F/Gas Mark 4. Grease two baking sheets.

2 Cream together the butter and sugar and whisk until light and fluffy. Sift together the flour, salt, bicarbonate of soda, cinnamon, coriander, nutmeg and cloves into the creamed mixture.

3 Stir the dark rum into the creamed mixture. Place 18 spoonfuls of the dough onto the prepared baking sheets, spaced well apart. Flatten each one slightly with the back of a spoon.

4 Bake in a preheated oven for 10–12 minutes until golden. Leave the biscuits to cool and crisp on wire racks before serving.

CHEQUERBOARDS

Makes about 20

- 225 g/8 oz butter, softened
- 140 g/5 oz caster sugar
- 1 egg yolk, lightly beaten
- 2 tsp vanilla extract
- 280 g/10 oz plain flour
- pinch of salt
- 1 tsp ground ginger
- 1 tbsp finely grated orange rind
- 1 tbsp cocoa powder
- 1 egg white, lightly beaten

1 Place the butter and sugar in a large bowl and beat together until light and fluffy, then beat in the egg yolk and vanilla extract. Sift together the flour and salt into the mixture and stir until combined.

2 Divide the dough in half. Add the ginger and orange rind to one half and mix well. Shape the dough into a log 15 cm/6 inches long. Flatten the sides and top to square off the log to 5 cm/2 inches high. Wrap in clingfilm and chill in the refrigerator for 30–60 minutes.

3 Sift the cocoa into the other half of the dough and mix well. Shape into a flattened log exactly the same size as the first one, wrap in clingfilm and chill in the refrigerator for 30–60 minutes.

4 Unwrap the two doughs and cut each log lengthways into three slices. Cut each slice lengthways into three strips. Brush the strips with egg white and stack them in threes, alternating the colours, so they are the same shape as the original logs. Wrap in clingfilm and chill for 30–60 minutes.

5 Preheat the oven to 190°C/375°F/Gas Mark 5. Line two large baking sheets with baking paper.

6 Unwrap the logs and cut into slices with a sharp serrated knife, then place the cookies on the prepared baking sheets, spaced well apart. Bake in the preheated oven for 12–15 minutes, or until firm. Leave to cool for 5–10 minutes, then transfer the cookies to wire racks to cool completely.

Santa
SUGAR COOKIES

Makes 40

- 350 g/12 oz plain flour, plus extra for dusting
- 1 tsp baking powder
- ¼ tsp salt
- 115 g/4 oz butter, softened, plus extra for greasing
- 175 g/6 oz caster sugar
- 1 egg, beaten
- 2½ tsp vanilla extract
- 1 tbsp milk

To decorate

- 225 g/8 oz icing sugar
- 1 egg white
- ½ tsp glycerine
- glycerine-based red and black food colouring

1 Grease four baking sheets. Sift together the flour, baking powder and salt together in a bowl. In a separate bowl, cream the butter and the caster sugar together until light and fluffy. Beat in the egg, 2 teaspoons of the vanilla extract and milk until smooth and then mix in the flour mixture to form a soft dough. Cover the dough with clingfilm and chill in the refrigerator for 30 minutes.

2 Preheat the oven to 180°C/350°F/Gas Mark 4. Roll out the chilled dough on a lightly floured work surface to 5 mm/¼ inch thick. Use a Santa-shaped cutter to cut out shapes from the dough. Transfer the cookies to the prepared baking sheets. Bake the cookies in the preheated oven for 10 minutes until golden brown. Remove from the oven and allow to cool for 5 minutes before transferring, using a palette knife, to a wire rack to cool completely.

3 Once the cookies are cool, whisk together the icing sugar, egg white, remaining vanilla extract and glycerine with an electric whisk for 5 minutes until stiff and glossy. Colour one third of the icing sugar mixture red and colour 2 tablespoons of the mixture black. Leave the rest of the mixture as white icing. Apply the red icing evenly with a small palette knife to create Santa's hat and pipe eyes in black icing using a fine nozzle.

4 Place the white icing in a piping bag fitted with a small star-shaped nozzle to create the fur cuff, eyebrows, moustache and bobble on Santa's hat. Apply the remainder of the icing using a swirling action with a small palette knife to create his beard. Leave to set for a few hours.

Reindeer
COOKIES

Makes 25

- 10 cardamom pods
- 100 g/3½ oz butter, softened, plus extra for greasing
- 55 g/2 oz caster sugar
- 1 egg, beaten
- finely grated rind of ½ orange
- 225 g/8 oz plain flour, plus extra for dusting
- 25 g/1 oz cornflour
- ½ tsp baking powder

To decorate

- 90 g/3¼ oz icing sugar
- 4 tsp lemon juice
- glycerine-based red food colouring
- 25 edible silver balls

1 Crush the cardamom pods lightly in a pestle and mortar and discard the shells. Grind the cardamom seeds to a powder. Beat together the butter and caster sugar in a bowl with a whisk until creamy, then gradually beat in the egg, orange rind and cardamom powder.

2 Sift together the flour, cornflour and baking powder into the mixture and stir with a wooden spoon to form a soft dough. Wrap the dough in clingfilm and chill in the refrigerator for 30 minutes.

3 Preheat the oven to 180°C/350°F/Gas Mark 4. Grease three baking sheets. Roll out the chilled dough on a lightly floured work surface to 3 mm/⅛ inch thick. Cut out shapes using a reindeer-shaped cutter, and place on the prepared baking sheets. Re-knead and re-roll trimmings and cut out more shapes until all the dough is used up.

4 Bake in the preheated oven for 15 minutes, until just golden. Allow to cool for 5 minutes before transferring to a wire rack to cool completely.

5 Mix together the icing sugar and lemon juice until smooth. Spoon 2 tablespoons of the mixture into a separate mixing bowl and colour it with the red food colouring. Spoon the rest of the icing into a piping bag fitted with a fine nozzle and pipe antlers, hooves, tail, collar and a saddle in white icing on the cookies. Pipe a nose using the red icing. For the eye, fix a silver ball using a blob of icing.

Sugar
COOKIE HEARTS

Makes about 30
- 225 g/8 oz butter, softened
- 280 g/10 oz caster sugar
- 1 egg yolk, lightly beaten
- 2 tsp vanilla extract
- 250 g/9 oz plain flour
- 25 g/1 oz cocoa powder
- pinch of salt
- 3–4 food colouring pastes
- 100 g/3½ oz plain chocolate, broken into pieces

1 Place the butter and half the sugar in a large bowl and beat together until light and fluffy, then beat in the egg yolk and vanilla extract. Sift together the flour, cocoa and salt into the mixture and stir until combined. Halve the dough, shape into balls, wrap in clingfilm and chill for 30–60 minutes.

2 Preheat the oven to 190°C/375°F/Gas Mark 5. Line two large baking sheets with baking paper. Unwrap the dough and roll out between two sheets of baking paper. Cut out cookies with a heart-shaped cutter and place them on the prepared baking sheets, spaced well apart. Bake in the preheated oven for 10–15 minutes, or until firm. Leave to cool on the baking sheets for 5–10 minutes, then transfer to wire racks to cool completely.

3 Meanwhile, divide the remaining sugar among four small plastic bags or bowls. Add a little food colouring paste to each and rub in until well mixed. Wear a plastic glove if mixing in bowls to prevent your hands from getting stained. Place the chocolate in a heatproof bowl, set the bowl over a saucepan of gently simmering water and heat until melted. Leave to cool slightly.

4 Leave the cookies on the racks. Spread the melted chocolate over them and sprinkle with the coloured sugar. Leave to set.

Cinnamon & Chocolate
CHIP COOKIES

Makes about 30

- 225 g/8 oz butter, softened
- 140 g/5 oz caster sugar
- 1 egg yolk, lightly beaten
- 2 tsp orange extract
- 280 g/10 oz plain flour
- pinch of salt
- 100 g/3½ oz plain chocolate chips

Cinnamon coating

- 1½ tbsp caster sugar
- 1½ tbsp ground cinnamon

1 Preheat the oven to 190°C/375°F/Gas Mark 5. Line two baking sheets with baking paper.

2 Put the butter and sugar into a bowl and mix well with a wooden spoon, then beat in the egg yolk and orange extract. Sift together the flour and salt into the mixture, add the chocolate chips and stir until thoroughly combined.

3 For the cinnamon coating, mix together the sugar and cinnamon in a shallow dish. Scoop out tablespoons of the cookie dough, roll them into balls, then roll them in the cinnamon mixture to coat. Flatten the cookies slightly with your fingers and put them on the prepared baking sheets, spaced well apart.

4 Bake in the preheated oven for 12–15 minutes. Leave to cool on the baking sheets for 5–10 minutes, then, using a palette knife, carefully transfer to wire racks to cool completely.

Cranberry & Coconut
COOKIES

Makes about 30

- 225 g/8 oz butter, softened
- 140 g/5 oz caster sugar
- 1 egg yolk, lightly beaten
- 2 tsp vanilla extract
- 280 g/10 oz plain flour
- pinch of salt
- 40 g/1½ oz desiccated coconut
- 60 g/2¼ oz dried cranberries

1 Preheat the oven to 190°C/375°F/Gas Mark 5. Line two baking sheets with baking paper.

2 Put the butter and sugar into a bowl and mix well with a wooden spoon, then beat in the egg yolk and vanilla extract. Sift together the flour and salt into the mixture, add the coconut and cranberries and stir until thoroughly combined. Scoop up tablespoons of the dough and place in mounds on the prepared baking sheets, spaced well apart.

3 Bake in the preheated oven for 12–15 minutes, until golden brown. Leave to cool on the baking sheets for 5–10 minutes, then, using a palette knife, carefully transfer to wire racks to cool completely.

Cookie
CANDY CANES

Makes 40

- 350 g/12 oz plain flour, plus extra for dusting
- 1 tsp bicarbonate of soda
- 100 g/3½ oz butter, softened, plus extra for greasing
- 175 g/6 oz soft brown sugar
- 1 egg, beaten
- 1 tsp vanilla extract
- 4 tbsp golden syrup

To decorate

- 450 g/1 lb icing sugar
- 135 ml/4½ fl oz lemon juice
- glycerine-based red food colouring

1 Preheat the oven to 180°C/350°F/Gas Mark 4. Grease three baking sheets.

2 Sift the flour and bicarbonate of soda together in a bowl. Add the butter and rub into the flour until the mixture resembles fine breadcrumbs, then stir in the brown sugar. In another bowl, beat together the egg, vanilla extract and golden syrup with a fork. Pour this mixture into the flour blend and stir to make a smooth dough, kneading lightly with your hands.

3 Roll the dough out on a lightly floured work surface to about 5 mm/¼ inch thick and cut into shapes using a candy cane-shaped cutter. Transfer the cookies to the prepared baking sheets. Bake in the preheated oven for 10 minutes, until golden brown. Remove the cookies from the oven and allow to cool for 5 minutes, before transferring, using a palette knife, to a wire rack to cool completely.

4 Once the cookies are cool, mix together 280 g/10 oz of the icing sugar and 75 ml/2½ fl oz of the lemon juice until smooth. Spoon the mixture into a piping bag fitted with a very fine nozzle and pipe the icing around the edge of the cookies. Empty any remaining icing into a small bowl, colour it with the red food colouring and cover with clingfilm. Mix the remaining icing sugar with the remaining lemon juice until smooth and runny. Spoon this into the centre of each cookie and encourage it to the piped edge to flood each biscuit. Allow to set overnight. Spoon the red icing into a piping bag fitted with a very fine nozzle and pipe stripes, dots and swirls over the dry iced cookies.

Cinnamon & Caramel
COOKIES

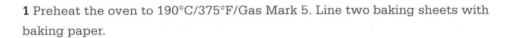

Makes about 25

- 225 g/8 oz butter, softened
- 140 g/5 oz caster sugar
- 1 egg yolk, lightly beaten
- 1 tsp vanilla extract
- 280 g/10 oz plain flour
- 1 tsp ground cinnamon
- ½ tsp mixed spice
- pinch of salt
- 25–30 caramel sweets

1 Preheat the oven to 190°C/375°F/Gas Mark 5. Line two baking sheets with baking paper.

2 Put the butter and sugar into a bowl and mix well with a wooden spoon, then beat in the egg yolk and vanilla extract. Sift together the flour, cinnamon, mixed spice and salt into the mixture and stir until thoroughly combined.

3 Scoop up tablespoons of the mixture, shape into balls and place on the prepared baking sheets, spaced well apart. Bake in the preheated oven for 8 minutes. Place a caramel sweet on top of each cookie, return to the oven and bake for a further 6–7 minutes.

4 Remove from the oven and leave to cool on the baking sheets for 5–10 minutes. Using a palette knife, carefully transfer the cookies to wire racks to cool completely.

Apple &
SPICE COOKIES

Makes about 30

- 225 g/8 oz butter, softened
- 140 g/5 oz caster sugar
- 1 egg yolk, lightly beaten
- 2 tsp apple juice
- 280 g/10 oz plain flour
- ½ tsp ground cinnamon
- ½ tsp mixed spice
- pinch of salt
- 100 g/3½ oz dried apple, finely chopped

Apple filling

- 1 tbsp caster sugar
- 1 tbsp custard powder
- 125 ml/4 fl oz milk
- 5 tbsp apple sauce

1 Put the butter and sugar into a bowl and mix well with a wooden spoon, then beat in the egg yolk and apple juice. Sift together the flour, cinnamon, mixed spice and salt into the mixture, add the dried apple and stir until thoroughly combined. Halve the dough, shape into balls, wrap in clingfilm and chill in the refrigerator for 30–60 minutes.

2 Preheat the oven to 190°C/375°F/Gas Mark 5. Line two baking sheets with baking paper.

3 Unwrap the dough and roll out between two sheets of baking paper. Stamp out cookies with a 5-cm/2-inch square cutter and put them on the prepared baking sheets, spaced well apart. Bake in the preheated oven for 10–15 minutes, until light golden brown. Leave to cool on the baking sheets for 5–10 minutes, then, using a palette knife, carefully transfer to wire racks to cool completely.

4 To make the apple filling, mix together the sugar, custard powder and milk in a saucepan and bring to the boil, stirring constantly. Cook, stirring constantly, until thickened, then remove the pan from the heat and stir in the apple sauce. Cover the surface with clingfilm and leave to cool.

5 Spread the filling over half the cookies and top with the remainder.

Christmas
BELLS

Makes about 30

- 225 g/8 oz butter, softened
- 140 g/5 oz caster sugar
- finely grated rind of 1 lemon
- 1 egg yolk, lightly beaten
- 280 g/10 oz plain flour
- ½ tsp ground cinnamon
- pinch of salt
- 100 g/3½ oz plain chocolate chips

To decorate

- 2 tbsp lightly beaten egg white
- 2 tbsp lemon juice
- 225 g/8 oz icing sugar
- 30 edible silver balls
- food colouring pens

1 Put the butter, caster sugar and lemon rind into a bowl and mix well with a wooden spoon, then beat in the egg yolk. Sift together the flour, cinnamon and salt into the mixture, add the chocolate chips and stir until thoroughly combined. Halve the dough, shape into balls, wrap in clingfilm and chill in the refrigerator for 30–60 minutes.

2 Preheat the oven to 190°C/375°F/Gas Mark 5. Line two baking sheets with baking paper.

3 Unwrap the dough and roll out between two sheets of baking paper. Stamp out cookies with a 5-cm/2-inch bell-shaped cutter and put them on the prepared baking sheets, spaced well apart.

4 Bake in the preheated oven for 10–15 minutes, until light golden brown. Leave to cool on the baking sheets for 5–10 minutes, then, using a palette knife, carefully transfer to wire racks to cool completely.

5 Mix together the egg white and lemon juice in a bowl, then gradually beat in the icing sugar until smooth. Leave the cookies on the racks and spread the icing over them. Place a silver ball on the clapper shape at the bottom of the cookie and leave to set completely. When the icing is dry, use the food colouring pens to draw patterns on the cookies.

Date & Lemon
SPIRALS

Makes about 30

- 225 g/8 oz butter, softened
- 175 g/6 oz caster sugar
- 1 egg yolk, lightly beaten
- 1 tsp lemon extract
- 280 g/10 oz plain flour
- pinch of salt
- 280 g/10 oz dried dates, stoned and finely chopped
- 2 tbsp clear lemon blossom honey
- 5 tbsp lemon juice
- 1 tbsp finely grated lemon rind
- 1 tsp ground cinnamon

1 Put the butter and 140 g/5 oz of the sugar into a bowl and mix well with a wooden spoon, then beat in the egg yolk and lemon extract. Sift together the flour and salt into the mixture and stir until thoroughly combined. Shape the dough into a ball, wrap in clingfilm and chill in the refrigerator for 30–60 minutes.

2 Meanwhile, put the dates, honey, lemon juice and lemon rind in a saucepan and stir in 125 ml/4 fl oz of water. Bring to the boil, stirring constantly, then lower the heat and simmer gently, stirring occasionally, for 5 minutes. Remove from the heat and leave to cool, then chill in the refrigerator for 15 minutes.

3 Mix together the cinnamon and remaining sugar in a bowl. Unwrap the dough and roll out between two sheets of baking paper into a 30-cm/12-inch square. Sprinkle the cinnamon and sugar mixture over the dough and roll lightly with the rolling pin. Spread the date mixture evenly over the dough, then roll up like a Swiss roll. Wrap in clingfilm and chill in the refrigerator for 30 minutes.

4 Preheat the oven to 190°C/375°F/Gas Mark 5. Line two baking sheets with baking paper. Unwrap the roll and cut into thin slices with a sharp serrated knife. Put them on the prepared baking sheets, spaced well apart. Bake in the preheated oven for 12–15 minutes, until golden brown. Leave to cool for 5–10 minutes, then transfer to wire racks to cool completely.

Cinnamon
STARS

Makes 20

- 2 egg whites
- 175 g/6 oz icing sugar,
  plus extra for dusting
- 250 g/9 oz ground hazelnuts,
  roasted
- 1 tbsp ground cinnamon

1 Whisk the egg whites in a clean dry bowl until stiff. Stir in the sugar until thoroughly combined and then continue to whisk until thick and glossy.

2 Remove 40 g/1½ oz of this mixture and set aside. Then fold the hazelnuts and cinnamon into the remaining mixture to make a very stiff dough. Chill in the refrigerator for about an hour.

3 Preheat the oven to 140°C/275°F/Gas Mark 1. Line two baking sheets with baking paper. Roll out the dough to 1 cm/½ inch thick on a surface amply floured with icing sugar.

4 Cut the dough into shapes using a 5-cm/2-inch star-shaped cutter, dusting with icing sugar to prevent sticking. Re-roll as necessary until all mixture is used up.

5 Place the cookies on the prepared baking sheets, spaced well apart, and spread the top of each star with the reserved egg white icing.

6 Bake in the preheated oven for 25 minutes, until the cookies are still white and crisp on top but slightly soft and moist underneath. Turn off the oven and open the oven door to release the heat and dry the cookies out in the oven for 10 more minutes. Transfer to wire racks to cool.

Blueberry, Cranberry & Cinnamon
COOKIES

Makes about 30
- 225 g/8 oz butter, softened
- 140 g/5 oz caster sugar
- 1 egg yolk, lightly beaten
- 2 tsp vanilla extract
- 280 g/10 oz plain flour
- 1 tsp ground cinnamon
- pinch of salt
- 55 g/2 oz dried blueberries
- 55 g/2 oz dried cranberries
- 55 g/2 oz pine kernels, chopped

1 Preheat the oven to 190°C/375°F/Gas Mark 5. Line two baking sheets with baking paper.

2 Put the butter and sugar into a bowl and mix well with a wooden spoon, then beat in the egg yolk and vanilla extract. Sift together the flour, cinnamon and salt into the mixture, add the blueberries and cranberries and stir until thoroughly combined.

3 Spread out the pine kernels in a shallow dish. Scoop up tablespoons of the mixture and roll them into balls. Roll the balls in the pine kernels to coat, then place on the prepared baking sheets, spaced well apart, and flatten slightly.

4 Bake in the preheated oven for 10–15 minutes. Leave to cool on the baking sheets for 5–10 minutes, then, using a palette knife, carefully transfer the cookies to wire racks to cool completely.

Apple Suns &
PEAR STARS

Makes about 30

- 225 g/8 oz butter, softened
- 140 g/5 oz caster sugar
- 1 egg yolk, lightly beaten
- 280 g/10 oz plain flour
- pinch of salt
- ½ tsp mixed spice
- 55 g/2 oz dried apple, finely chopped
- ½ tsp ground ginger
- 55 g/2 oz dried pear, finely chopped
- 25 g/1 oz flaked almonds
- 1 egg white, lightly beaten
- demerara sugar, for sprinkling

1 Put the butter and caster sugar into a bowl and mix well with a wooden spoon, then beat in the egg yolk. Sift together the flour and salt into the mixture and stir until thoroughly combined. Transfer half the dough to another bowl.

2 Add the mixed spice and dried apple to one bowl and mix well. Shape into a ball, wrap in clingfilm and chill in the refrigerator for 30–60 minutes. Add the ginger and dried pear to the other bowl and mix well. Shape into a ball, wrap in clingfilm and chill in the refrigerator for 30–60 minutes.

3 Preheat the oven to 190°C/375°F/Gas Mark 5. Line two baking sheets with baking paper.

4 Unwrap the apple-flavoured dough and roll out between two sheets of baking paper to about 3 mm/⅛ inch thick. Stamp out cookies with a sun-shaped cutter and put them on a prepared baking sheet. Repeat with the pear-flavoured dough and stamp out cookies with a star-shaped cutter. Put them on the other prepared baking sheet.

5 Bake in the preheated oven for 5 minutes, then remove the star-shaped cookies from the oven and sprinkle with the flaked almonds. Return to the oven and bake for a further 5–10 minutes. Remove the cookies from the oven but do not turn off the heat. Brush the apple suns with a little egg white and sprinkle with the demerara sugar. Return to the oven for 2–3 minutes. Leave all the cookies to cool for 5–10 minutes, then carefully transfer them to wire racks to cool completely.

White Chocolate &
PLUM COOKIES

Makes about 30

- 225 g/8 oz butter, softened
- 140 g/5 oz caster sugar
- 1 egg yolk, lightly beaten
- 2 tsp vanilla extract
- 225 g/8 oz plain flour
- 55 g/2 oz cocoa powder
- pinch of salt
- 100 g/3½ oz white chocolate, chopped

To decorate
- 55 g/2 oz white chocolate, broken into pieces
- 15 dried plums, halved

1 Put the butter and sugar into a bowl and mix well with a wooden spoon, then beat in the egg yolk and vanilla extract. Sift together the flour, cocoa and salt into the mixture and stir until thoroughly combined. Halve the dough, shape into balls, wrap in clingfilm and chill in the refrigerator for 30–60 minutes.

2 Preheat the oven to 190°C/375°F/Gas Mark 5. Line two baking sheets with baking paper. Unwrap a ball of dough and roll out between two sheets of baking paper to about 3 mm/⅛ inch thick. Stamp out 15 rounds with a plain 5-cm/2-inch cutter and put them on the prepared baking sheets, spaced well apart. Divide the chopped chocolate among the cookies. Roll out the remaining dough between two sheets of baking paper and stamp out rounds with a 6–7-cm/2½–2¾-inch cutter. Place them on top of the first cookies and press the edges together to seal.

3 Bake in the preheated oven for 10–15 minutes, until firm. Leave to cool for 5–10 minutes, then carefully transfer the cookies to wire racks to cool completely. To decorate, melt the chocolate in a heatproof bowl set over a pan of gently simmering water. Remove from the heat and leave to cool slightly. Leave the cookies on the racks. Dip the cut sides of the plums into the melted chocolate and stick them in the middle of the cookies. Spoon the remaining melted chocolate over them and leave to set.

Walnut & Fig
PINWHEELS

Makes about 30
- 225 g/8 oz butter, softened
- 200 g/7 oz caster sugar
- 1 egg yolk, lightly beaten
- 225 g/8 oz plain flour
- pinch of salt
- 55 g/2 oz ground walnuts
- 280 g/10 oz dried figs,
  finely chopped
- 5 tbsp freshly brewed mint tea
- 2 tsp finely chopped fresh mint

1 Put the butter and 140 g/5 oz of the sugar into a bowl and mix well with a wooden spoon, then beat in the egg yolk. Sift together the flour and salt into the mixture, add the ground walnuts and stir until thoroughly combined. Shape the dough into a ball, wrap in clingfilm and chill in the refrigerator for 30–60 minutes.

2 Meanwhile, put the remaining sugar into a saucepan and stir in 125 ml/ 4 fl oz of water, then add the figs, mint tea and chopped mint. Bring to the boil, stirring constantly, until the sugar has dissolved, then lower the heat and simmer gently, stirring occasionally, for 5 minutes. Remove the pan from the heat and leave to cool.

3 Unwrap the dough and roll out between two sheets of baking paper into a 30-cm/12-inch square. Spread the fig filling evenly over the dough, then roll up like a Swiss roll. Wrap in clingfilm and chill in the refrigerator for 30 minutes.

4 Preheat the oven to 190°C/375°F/Gas Mark 5. Line two baking sheets with baking paper. Unwrap the roll and cut into thin slices with a sharp serrated knife. Put the slices on the prepared baking sheets, spaced well apart. Bake in the preheated oven for 10–15 minutes, until golden brown. Leave to cool on the baking sheets for 5–10 minutes, then, using a palette knife, transfer to wire racks to cool completely.

Christmas
TREE COOKIES

Makes 12

- 150 g/5½ oz plain flour, plus extra for dusting
- 1 tsp ground cinnamon
- ½ tsp ground nutmeg
- ½ tsp ground ginger
- 70 g/2½ oz unsalted butter, softened, plus extra for greasing
- 3 tbsp honey

To decorate
- white icing (optional)
- edible coloured balls

1 Sift the flour and spices into a bowl and rub in the butter until the mixture resembles breadcrumbs. Add the honey and mix together well to form a soft dough. Wrap the dough in clingfilm and chill in the refrigerator for 30 minutes.

2 Meanwhile, preheat the oven to 180°C/350°F/Gas Mark 4 and grease two baking sheets. Divide the dough in half. Roll out one piece of dough on a floured work surface to about 5 mm/¼ inch thick. Cut out tree shapes using a cutter or cardboard template. Repeat with the remaining piece of dough.

3 Put the cookies on the prepared baking sheets and, using a skewer, make a hole through the top of each biscuit large enough to thread the ribbon through. Chill in the refrigerator for 15 minutes.

4 Bake in the preheated oven for 10–12 minutes, until golden. Leave to cool on the baking sheets for 5 minutes, then transfer to a wire rack to cool completely. Decorate the trees with white icing and coloured balls, or simply leave them plain, then thread a length of ribbon through each hole and knot. Hang from the Christmas tree.

49

Stained-glass Window
COOKIES

Makes about 25

- 350 g/12 oz plain flour,
  plus extra for dusting
- pinch of salt
- 1 tsp bicarbonate of soda
- 100 g/3½ oz unsalted butter,
  softened
- 175 g/6 oz caster sugar
- 1 large egg
- 1 tsp vanilla extract
- 4 tbsp golden syrup
- 50 mixed coloured boiled fruit
  sweets (about 250 g/9 oz),
  chopped

1 Sift the flour, salt and bicarbonate of soda into a large bowl, add the butter
and rub it in until the mixture resembles breadcrumbs. Stir in the sugar.
Place the egg, vanilla extract and golden syrup in a separate bowl and whisk
together. Pour the egg into the flour mixture and mix to form a smooth dough.
Wrap in clingfilm and chill in the refrigerator for 30 minutes.

2 Preheat the oven to 180°C/350°F/Gas Mark 4. Line two large baking sheets
with baking paper. Roll the dough out on a floured work surface to 5 mm/
¼ inch thick. Use a variety of floured cookie cutter shapes to cut out shapes.

3 Transfer the shapes to the prepared baking sheets and cut out shapes from
the centre of the cookies. Fill the holes with the sweets. Using a skewer, make
a hole in the top of each cookie.

4 Bake in the preheated oven for 10–12 minutes, or until the sweets are melted.
Make sure the holes are still there, and re-pierce if necessary. Leave to cool
on the baking sheets until the centres have hardened. When cold, thread thin
ribbon through the holes to hang up the cookies.

Spiced
FRUIT COOKIES

Makes about 30
- 225 g/8 oz butter, softened
- 140 g/5 oz caster sugar
- 1 egg yolk, lightly beaten
- 280 g/10 oz plain flour
- ½ tsp mixed spice
- pinch of salt
- 25 g/1 oz dried apple, chopped
- 25 g/1 oz dried pear, chopped
- 25 g/1 oz prunes, chopped
- grated rind of 1 orange

1 Put the butter and sugar into a bowl and mix well with a wooden spoon, then beat in the egg yolk. Sift together the flour, mixed spice and salt into the mixture, add the apple, pear, prunes and orange rind and stir until thoroughly combined. Shape the dough into a log, wrap in clingfilm and chill in the refrigerator for 30–60 minutes.

2 Preheat the oven to 190°C/375°F/Gas Mark 5. Line two baking sheets with baking paper.

3 Unwrap the log and cut it into 5-mm/¼-inch thick slices with a sharp serrated knife. Put them on the prepared baking sheets, spaced well apart.

4 Bake in the preheated oven for 10–15 minutes, until golden brown. Leave to cool on the baking sheets for 5–10 minutes, then, using a palette knife, carefully transfer the cookies to wire racks to cool completely.

GINGER SNAPS

Makes 30

- 350 g/12 oz self-raising flour
- pinch of salt
- 200 g/7 oz caster sugar
- 1 tbsp ground ginger
- 1 tsp bicarbonate of soda
- 125 g/4½ oz butter, plus extra for greasing
- 75 g/2¾ oz golden syrup
- 1 egg, beaten
- 1 tsp grated orange rind

1 Preheat the oven to 160°C/325°F/Gas Mark 3. Grease two baking sheets.

2 Sift together the flour, salt, sugar, ginger and bicarbonate of soda into a large mixing bowl.

3 Heat the butter and golden syrup together in a saucepan over a very low heat until the butter has melted. Remove the pan from the heat and leave to cool slightly, then pour the contents onto the dry ingredients. Add the egg and orange rind and mix thoroughly to form a dough. Using your hands, carefully shape the dough into 30 even-sized balls.

4 Place the balls on the prepared baking sheets, spaced well apart, and flatten slightly with your fingers.

5 Bake in the preheated oven for 15–20 minutes, then carefully transfer to wire racks to cool.

Christmas Tree
DECORATIONS

Makes 20–25

- 225 g/8 oz butter, softened
- 140 g/5 oz caster sugar
- 1 egg yolk, lightly beaten
- 2 tsp vanilla extract
- 280 g/10 oz plain flour
- pinch of salt
- 1 egg white, lightly beaten
- 2 tbsp hundreds-and-thousands
- 400 g/14 oz mixed coloured boiled fruit sweets

1 Put the butter and sugar into a bowl and mix well with a wooden spoon, then beat in the egg yolk and vanilla extract. Sift together the flour and salt into the mixture and stir until thoroughly combined. Halve the dough, shape into balls, wrap in clingfilm and chill in the refrigerator for 30–60 minutes. Preheat the oven to 190°C/375°F/Gas Mark 5. Line two baking sheets with baking paper.

2 Unwrap the dough and roll out between two sheets of baking paper. Stamp out cookies with Christmas-themed cutters and put them on the prepared baking sheets, spaced well apart. Using the end of a large plain piping nozzle, stamp out rounds from each shape and remove them. Make a small hole in the top of each cookie with a skewer so that they can be threaded with ribbon. Brush with egg white and sprinkle with hundreds-and-thousands. Bake in the preheated oven for 7 minutes.

3 Meanwhile, lightly crush the sweets by tapping them with a rolling pin. Unwrap and sort into separate bowls by colour. Remove the cookies from the oven and fill the holes with the crushed sweets. Return to the oven and bake for a further 5–8 minutes, until the cookies are light golden brown and the sweets have melted and filled the holes. Leave to cool. Thread thin ribbon through the holes in the top and hang.

Holly
LEAF COOKIES

Makes 30

- 55 g/2 oz butter, softened,
  plus extra for greasing
- 85 g/3 oz caster sugar
- 1 egg yolk
- ⅛ tsp almond extract
- 115 g/4 oz plain flour,
  plus extra for dusting
- 2 tsp milk
- 85 g/3 oz boiled sweets

1 Cream the butter and sugar together in a bowl until light and fluffy. Beat in the egg yolk and almond extract until smooth and then sift in the flour and add the milk to produce a soft dough. Cover with clingfilm and allow to chill in the refrigerator for 30 minutes.

2 Preheat the oven to 180°C/350°F/Gas Mark 4. Grease two baking sheets. Crush the sweets by tapping them with a rolling pin. Roll out the chilled dough on a lightly floured work surface to 5 mm/¼ inch thick.

3 Use a large holly leaf-shaped cutter to cut out shapes from the dough and then use a smaller holly-shaped cutter to cut out and remove the middle of each larger holly shape.

4 Using a skewer, cut a small hole out of the top of each cookie so they can be threaded with ribbon. Re-knead and re-roll the dough trimmings and cut out until all the dough is used up. Place all the holly shapes on the prepared baking sheets.

5 Divide the crushed boiled sweet pieces evenly to fill the holes in the middle of the cookies. Bake in the preheated oven for 8–10 minutes until the cookies are just turning golden around the edges.

6 When completely cool, transfer the cookies, using a palette knife, to a wire rack. Thread thin ribbon through the holes and hang.

Peach, Pear &
PLUM COOKIES

Makes about 30

- 225 g/8 oz butter, softened
- 140 g/5 oz caster sugar
- 1 egg yolk, lightly beaten
- 2 tsp almond extract
- 280 g/10 oz plain flour
- pinch of salt
- 55 g/2 oz dried peach, finely chopped
- 55 g/2 oz dried pear, finely chopped
- 4 tbsp plum jam

1 Preheat the oven to 190°C/375°F/Gas Mark 5. Line two baking sheets with baking paper.

2 Put the butter and sugar into a bowl and mix well with a wooden spoon, then beat in the egg yolk and almond extract. Sift together the flour and salt into the mixture, add the dried fruit and stir until thoroughly combined.

3 Scoop up tablespoons of the mixture, roll them into balls and place on the prepared baking sheets, spaced well apart. Make a hollow in the centre of each with the dampened handle of a wooden spoon. Fill the hollows with the jam.

4 Bake in the preheated oven for 12–15 minutes, until light golden brown. Leave to cool on the baking sheets for 5–10 minutes, then, using a palette knife, carefully transfer to wire racks to cool completely.

Iced
STARS

Makes 30

- 225 g/8 oz butter, softened
- 140 g/5 oz caster sugar
- 1 egg yolk, lightly beaten
- ½ tsp vanilla extract
- 280 g/10 oz plain flour
- pinch of salt

To decorate
- 200 g/7 oz icing sugar
- 1–2 tbsp warm water
- food colourings
- edible silver and gold balls
- hundreds-and-thousands
- sugar sprinkles
- sugar stars, hearts and flowers
- desiccated coconut

1 Place the butter and caster sugar in a large bowl and beat together until light and fluffy, then beat in the egg yolk and vanilla extract. Sift together the flour and salt into the mixture and stir until thoroughly combined. Halve the dough, shape into balls, wrap in clingfilm and chill in the refrigerator for 30–60 minutes.

2 Preheat the oven to 190°C/375°F/Gas Mark 5. Line two large baking sheets with baking paper.

3 Unwrap the dough and roll out between two sheets of baking paper to about 3 mm/⅛ inch thick. Cut out cookies with a star-shaped cutter and place them on the prepared baking sheets, spaced well apart. Bake in the preheated oven for 10–15 minutes, or until light golden brown. Leave to cool on the baking sheets for 5–10 minutes, then transfer to wire racks to cool completely.

4 To decorate, sift the icing sugar into a bowl and stir in enough warm water until it is the consistency of thick cream. Divide the icing among 3–4 bowls and add a few drops of your chosen food colourings to each. Leave the cookies on the racks and spread the different coloured icings over them to the edges. Arrange silver and gold balls on top and/or sprinkle with hundreds-and-thousands and sugar shapes. If you like, colour desiccated coconut with food colouring in a contrasting colour and sprinkle over the cookies. Leave to set.

Christmas
GIFT COOKIES

Makes about 30

- 225 g/8 oz butter, softened
- 140 g/5 oz caster sugar
- 1 egg yolk, lightly beaten
- 2 tsp orange juice or orange liqueur
- finely grated rind of 1 orange
- 280 g/10 oz plain flour
- pinch of salt

To decorate

- 1 egg white
- 225 g/8 oz icing sugar
- few drops each of 2 food colourings
- edible silver balls

1 Place the butter and caster sugar in a large bowl and beat together until light and fluffy, then beat in the egg yolk, orange juice and grated rind. Sift together the flour and salt into the mixture and stir until combined. Halve the dough, shape into balls, wrap in clingfilm and chill in the refrigerator for 30–60 minutes.

2 Preheat the oven to 190°C/375°F/Gas Mark 5. Line two large baking sheets with baking paper. Unwrap the dough and roll out to 3 mm/⅛ inch thick. Cut out appropriate shapes, such as stars or Christmas trees, with cookie cutters and place them on the baking sheets, spaced well apart. Bake in the preheated oven for 10–15 minutes, or until light golden brown.

3 Leave to cool on the baking sheets for 5–10 minutes, then transfer the cookies to wire racks to cool completely.

4 Leave the cookies on the racks. Put the egg white and icing sugar into a bowl and beat until smooth, adding a little water if necessary. Transfer half the icing to another bowl and colour each bowl with a different colour. Put both icings in piping bags with fine nozzles and use to decorate the cookies and write the initials of the person who will receive the cookies as a gift. Finish with silver balls and leave to set.

Cinnamon
ORANGE CRISPS

Makes about 30

- 225 g/8 oz butter, softened
- 200 g/7 oz caster sugar
- finely grated rind of 1 orange
- 1 egg yolk, lightly beaten
- 4 tsp orange juice
- 280 g/10 oz plain flour
- pinch of salt
- 2 tsp ground cinnamon

1 Place the butter, 140 g/5 oz of the sugar and the orange rind in a large bowl and beat together until light and fluffy, then beat in the egg yolk and 2 teaspoons of the orange juice. Sift together the flour and salt into the mixture and stir until thoroughly combined. Shape the dough into a ball, wrap in clingfilm and chill in the refrigerator for 30–60 minutes.

2 Unwrap the dough and roll out between two sheets of baking paper into a 30-cm/12-inch square. Brush with the remaining orange juice and sprinkle with the remaining sugar and cinnamon. Lightly roll with the rolling pin. Roll up the dough like a Swiss roll. Wrap in clingfilm and chill for 30 minutes.

3 Preheat the oven to 190°C/375°F/Gas Mark 5. Line two large baking sheets with baking paper.

4 Unwrap the dough and cut into thin slices, then place on the prepared baking sheets, spaced well apart. Bake in the preheated oven for 10–12 minutes. Leave to cool for 5–10 minutes, then transfer to wire racks to cool completely.

Christmas
ANGELS

Makes about 25

- 225 g/8 oz butter, softened
- 140 g/5 oz caster sugar
- 1 egg yolk, lightly beaten
- 2 tsp passion fruit pulp
- 280 g/10 oz plain flour
- pinch of salt
- 55 g/2 oz desiccated coconut

To decorate
- 175 g/6 oz icing sugar
- 1–1½ tbsp passion fruit pulp
- edible silver glitter, for sprinkling

1 Put the butter and caster sugar into a bowl and mix well with a wooden spoon, then beat in the egg yolk and passion fruit pulp. Sift together the flour and salt into the mixture, add the coconut and stir until thoroughly combined. Halve the dough, shape into balls, wrap in clingfilm and chill in the refrigerator for 30–60 minutes.

2 Preheat the oven to 190°C/375°F/Gas Mark 5. Line two baking sheets with baking paper.

3 Unwrap the dough and roll out between two sheets of baking paper. Stamp out cookies with a 7-cm/2¾-inch angel-shaped cutter and put them on the prepared baking sheets, spaced well apart.

4 Bake in the preheated oven for 10–15 minutes, until light golden brown. Leave to cool on the baking sheets for 5–10 minutes, then, using a palette knife, carefully transfer to wire racks to cool completely.

5 Sift the icing sugar into a bowl and stir in the passion fruit pulp until the icing has the consistency of thick cream. Leave the cookies on the racks and spread the icing over them. Sprinkle with the edible glitter and leave to set.

Chocolate, Date & Pecan Nut
PINWHEELS

Makes about 30

- 225 g/8 oz butter, softened
- 200 g/7 oz caster sugar
- 1 egg yolk, lightly beaten
- 225 g/8 oz plain flour
- 55 g/2 oz cocoa powder
- pinch of salt
- 100 g/3½ oz pecan nuts, finely ground
- 280 g/10 oz dried dates, stoned and roughly chopped
- finely grated rind of 1 orange
- 175 ml/6 fl oz orange flower water

1 Place the butter and 140 g/5 oz of the sugar in a large bowl and beat together until light and fluffy, then beat in the egg yolk. Sift together the flour, cocoa and salt into the mixture, add the nuts and stir until combined. Halve the dough, shape into balls, wrap in clingfilm and chill in the refrigerator for 30–60 minutes.

2 Meanwhile, place the dates, orange rind, orange flower water and remaining sugar into a saucepan and cook over a low heat, stirring, until the sugar has dissolved. Bring to the boil, then reduce the heat and simmer, for 5 minutes. Pour the mixture into a bowl, cool, then chill.

3 Unwrap the dough and roll out between two sheets of baking paper to rectangles 5 mm/¼ inch thick. Spread the filling over the rectangles and roll up like a Swiss roll. Wrap in the paper and chill in the refrigerator for 30 minutes. Preheat the oven to 190°C/375°F/Gas Mark 5. Line two large baking sheets with baking paper. Unwrap the rolls, cut into 1-cm/½-inch slices and place them on the prepared baking sheets.

4 Bake in the preheated oven for 15–20 minutes, or until golden brown. Leave to cool on the baking sheets for 5–10 minutes, then transfer the cookies to wire racks to cool completely.

German
LEBKUCHEN

....

Makes 60

- 3 eggs
- 200 g/7 oz caster sugar
- 55 g/2 oz plain flour
- 2 tsp cocoa powder
- 1 tsp ground cinnamon
- ½ tsp ground cardamom
- ¼ tsp ground cloves
- ¼ tsp ground nutmeg
- 175 g/6 oz ground almonds
- 55 g/2 oz mixed peel, finely chopped

To decorate
- 115 g/4 oz plain chocolate, broken into pieces
- 115 g/4 oz white chocolate, broken into pieces
- sugar crystals

1 Preheat the oven to 180°C/350°F/Gas Mark 4. Line several large baking sheets with baking paper. Place the eggs and sugar in a heatproof bowl set over a saucepan of gently simmering water and whisk until thick and foamy. Remove the bowl from the pan and continue to whisk for 2 minutes.

2 Sift the flour, cocoa, cinnamon, cardamom, cloves and nutmeg into the bowl and stir in with the ground almonds and mixed peel. Drop heaped teaspoonfuls of the mixture onto the prepared baking sheets, spreading them gently into smooth mounds.

3 Bake in the preheated oven for 15–20 minutes, or until light brown and slightly soft to the touch. Leave to cool on the baking sheets for 10 minutes, then transfer the cookies to wire racks to cool completely.

4 Place the plain and white chocolate in two separate heatproof bowls, set the bowls over two pans of gently simmering water and heat until melted. Dip half the biscuits in the melted plain chocolate and half in the white chocolate. Sprinkle with sugar crystals and leave to set.

Treacle & Spice
DRIZZLES

Makes about 25

- 200 g/7 oz butter, softened
- 2 tbsp black treacle
- 140 g/5 oz caster sugar
- 1 egg yolk, lightly beaten
- 280 g/10 oz plain flour
- 1 tsp ground cinnamon
- ½ tsp grated nutmeg
- ½ tsp ground cloves
- pinch of salt
- 2 tbsp chopped walnuts

To decorate

- 115 g/4 oz icing sugar
- 1 tbsp hot water
- a few drops of yellow food colouring
- a few drops of pink food colouring

1 Put the butter, treacle and caster sugar into a bowl and mix well with a wooden spoon, then beat in the egg yolk. Sift together the flour, cinnamon, nutmeg, cloves and salt into the mixture, add the walnuts and stir until thoroughly combined. Halve the dough, shape into balls, wrap in clingfilm and chill in the refrigerator for 30–60 minutes.

2 Preheat the oven to 190°C/375°F/Gas Mark 5. Line two baking sheets with baking paper.

3 Unwrap the dough and roll out between two sheets of baking paper to about 5 mm/¼ inch thick. Stamp out rounds with a 6-cm/2½-inch fluted cutter and put them on the prepared baking sheets.

4 Bake in the preheated oven for 10–15 minutes, until firm. Leave to cool on the baking sheets for 5–10 minutes, then, using a palette knife, carefully transfer the cookies to wire racks to cool completely.

5 For the icing, sift the icing sugar into a bowl, then gradually stir in the hot water until the icing has the consistency of thick cream. Spoon half the icing into another bowl and stir a few drops of yellow food colouring into one bowl and a few drops of pink food colouring into the other. Leave the cookies on the racks and, using teaspoons, drizzle the yellow icing over them in one direction and the pink icing over them at right angles. Leave to set.

Silver
STAR COOKIES

Makes 36

- 175 g/6 oz plain flour, plus extra for dusting
- 1 tsp ground cinnamon
- 1 tsp ground ginger
- 90 g/3¼ oz butter, softened
- 85 g/3 oz soft light brown sugar
- finely grated rind of 1 orange
- 1 egg, lightly beaten

To decorate
- 200 g/7 oz icing sugar
- 3–4 tsp cold water
- edible silver cake sparkles
- edible silver balls

1 Preheat the oven to 180°C/350°F/Gas Mark 4. Line several large baking sheets with baking paper.

2 Sift the flour, cinnamon and ginger into a large bowl. Add the butter and rub it in with your fingertips until the mixture resembles fine breadcrumbs. Stir the brown sugar and orange rind into the mixture, add the egg and mix together to form a soft dough.

3 Roll the mixture out thinly to about 5 mm/¼ inch thick on a lightly floured work surface. Cut out shapes with a 6.5-cm/2½-inch snowflake- or star-shaped cutter and place on the prepared baking sheets.

4 Bake in the preheated oven for 10–15 minutes, or until golden brown. Leave to cool on the baking sheets for 2–3 minutes, then transfer the cookies to a wire rack and leave to cool completely.

5 To make the icing, sift the icing sugar into a large bowl and add enough cold water to make a smooth, thick icing. Spread a little on each cookie and then sprinkle with sparkles and silver balls.

Christmas Stocking
COOKIES

Makes 30

- 100 g/3½ oz butter, plus extra for greasing
- 55 g/2 oz caster sugar
- 1 egg, beaten
- finely grated rind and juice of 1 lemon
- 225 g/8 oz plain flour, plus extra for dusting
- 25 g/1 oz cornflour, plus extra for dusting
- ½ tsp baking powder
- 1 tbsp mixed spice

To decorate
- 250 g/9 oz ready-to-roll fondant icing
- glycerine-based red and green food colouring
- 280 g/10 oz icing sugar
- 1 egg white
- ½ tsp glycerine

1 Beat together the butter and caster sugar in a bowl with a whisk until creamy. Then gradually beat in the egg and lemon rind. Sift together the flour, cornflour, baking powder and mixed spice into the mixture and stir to combine thoroughly into a soft dough. Wrap in clingfilm and chill in the refrigerator for 30 minutes.

2 Preheat the oven to 180°C/350°F/Gas Mark 4. Grease two baking sheets. Roll out on a lightly floured work surface to 5 mm/¼ inch thick. Using a Christmas stocking-shaped cutter, cut out shapes from the dough and place on the prepared baking sheets. Re-knead and re-roll trimmings and cut out until all the dough is used up. Bake in the preheated oven for 15 minutes, until just golden. Allow to cool for 5 minutes, before transferring to a wire rack to cool.

3 Mix the green colouring into 25 g/1 oz fondant icing, adding a little icing sugar until well blended. Cover to prevent drying out. Repeat with remaining fondant icing and the red food colouring. Roll out the green fondant icing as thinly as possible on a surface lightly dusted in cornflour and cut out shapes using a small holly-leaf cutter. Set aside. Roll out the red fondant icing, again as thinly as possible. Cut out shapes using the Christmas stocking-shaped cutter. Stick each stocking to the cookie by using a little lemon juice.

4 Whisk together the remaining icing sugar, egg white and glycerine for 5 minutes with an electric whisk until stiff and glossy. Slacken the mixture if needed with a little lemon juice to make it thick, but still possible to pipe. Fill a piping bag, fitted with a small star-shaped nozzle, with this icing sugar mixture. Pipe rows of stars to form a furry cuff on each stocking. Stick a holly-leaf shape into the piped icing on each cookie. Leave to set.